Wanton Disarray

Michelle Hartman

Wanton Disarray

Michelle Hartman

Hungry Buzzard Press — 2019

Copyrignt 2018 Michelle Hartman

All rights reserved. This book or any portion thereof may not be reproduced or used in any manner whatsoever without the express written permission of the publisher except for the use of brief quotations in a book review or scholarly journal.

First Printing: 2019

ISBN: ISBN-13: 978-0-578-21801-4

(Hungry Buzzard Press)

ISBN-10: 0-578-21801-1

Published by:

Hungry Buzzard Press
4669 Mountain Oak St.
Fort Worth, TX 76244

Front cover photo courtesy of William Neil Drake

This book is lovingly dedicated to Wesley

for now and forever.

Acknowledgements

Poems in this book have appeared
in the following publications;

San Pedro River Review
Melusine
Dragon Poet Review
Plainsongs
The Galway Review, (Ireland)
Panoplyzine
Blue Hole Anthology
Five Poetry Journal, (Australia)
Illya's Honey
La Noria
First Literary Review-East
Dallas Review, formerly, Sojourn
Picaroon Poetry
Muddy River Poetry Journal
Floyd County Moonshine
Red Eft Review
The Enigmatist
Suisun Valley Review
The Chaffin Journal
CALYX, A Journal of Art and Literature by Women
Better Than Starbucks
Concho River Review
Hot Summer Nights Anthology

Table of Contents

If 11
Touch and Gos 13
    Break-ups come before 15
    Caoinim* 16
    We dance round 17
    Saddest places 18
    Everywhere you look 19
    M dashes cause cancer 20
    Weddings & death 21
    Autopsy 22
    Autumn did not come this year 23
    What came first, the chicken 24
    The best way to a man's heart 26
    she sculpted 27
    After many a summer dies the swan 28
    Can't 29
    Hope has no conscience 30
    pourri means rotten in French 31
    A green removal van or why I cannot love you 32
Fleeting kisses 33
    The neon invite 35
    Common sense packed a bag on the third cocktail 36
    New lover 37
    Love poems for cannibals 38
    Spaceman Dave 39
    Moment 40
    Clay bodies 41
    don't remember when 42
    Editorial 43
    By the way 44

A rose by	45
Magic	46
the eastern clouds	47
I have no dowry	48
If by chance	49
Behavior of waves	50
Wanton Disarray	51
All I want is a kiss	53
before I drown in life	54
When I'm alone	56
Bookstore	57
Fall, falling, fell	58
I have met a regrettable for instance	59
All he said was hello	60
The first time	61
Mother said I would be safe	62
Practice	63
Snow	64
#2	65
The days go by	66
in a frenzied moment	68
I must wake you	69
Hold and kiss me until the dawn	70
But when I kiss you	71
Birds and bees, Part 2	72
an Giblean*	73
Didn't know I was starving until I tasted you	74
Appetites vary	75
Where two curves meet	76
A poetic light	77
Bolt from the blue	78

Speaking of boiled eggs	79
It's been too long	80
hunting	81
How invisibility works	82
champagne shoulders	83
A ticklish thing, anticipation	84
Headlong	86
Whimsy	87
I find it easy	88
Singing in the dark	89
She asked what you are like	90
Those who wander are not lost	91
Of Christmases to come	92
About the author	94

If

I.

      you are worried about custom
expectation or performance
and especially
body hair, underwear
or age of sheets

are trying to justify
reason, are already
working on excuses

have questions to ask
logistics to ponder.

This is not your time.

II.

      you think the heat from your loins
should be able to warm
the room as immersion heater

it's exotic and familiar

life has become barb wire
    hung with diamonds
rusted iron sprinkled
    with star dust

white powder and rusty metal
    heat building until they ignite.

That collective sigh
through the Cosmos
says this is your time.

Touch and Gos

That is the land of lost content,
I see it shining plain,
The happy highways where I went
And cannot come again.

Alfred E. Housman (1859 – 1936)

Break-ups come before

A few find their intended
sharing a crayon in Pre-K
a Junior High, mud puddle mishap
or setting behind them in algebra.

But the rest and sadly
majority must wander
a cobblestone ice highway.

Experiencing rambling mounds
of candy floss to the empty
eyes of an old snake.

Meet   Fall   Run
Repeat

Before we meet the person,
who makes us believe
the North wind is violet
and the South wind
the color of angels crying.

Caoinim*

    from without
old darknesses

      Shallow add — hits—
         lies now with
buried truth, slink

      through showdown
our love wears

a large target

*Gaelic for "I wail" origin of the word Keen.

We dance round

    & round
I in my ballgown
    he in a tux.
The mirror panels
show many couples
twirling
& when the light
    goes away, I wait
in darkness for him
    to speak, touch
but he is obsessed
with the man
    in the mirror

Saddest places

Inside a bar is everything
      we might reasonably regret later.

But the parking lot is
      the saddest place in town.
You're too sober for reality
and exiting you're too
drunk to drive or well…
anything.

A temporal zone
      of puke, piss, & potential

emotions are locked
in a Schrodinger's conundrum.

Time watches from
the shadows
& coughs
when you would renege
on that long & loathsome walk.

Broken neon sign blinks
The Feisty Bull

Everywhere you look

      are echoes, memories
crumbling brick, shuttered doors

these old halls shrug up
their secrets   wear them
     ignoble state of carelessness

creeping light
    fractured windows
creates thin beams, lace floor
      with scattered white poles

air inside a soup of color
old fires' carbon
    urine
       dust with hint of old flour

this must be where
old Mediums, hair pins
     & dead birds go

had Death, himself, that
unbelievable concept

hired a realtor this
would be first spot
he'd be shown

& even then
found too cheerless

this place with fate's
scars reminds me
a poem is a mirror

M dashes cause cancer

The Poet's life
has a stanza break
assuming something
    afterwords.

Years spent wallowing
in permanent crepuscular miasma
of mental shadow,
    stench of sweat
        tobacco, and booze
making it unhealthy, dangerous
in equal degrees.

Expressing our desires
in Virgilian Hexameters
regarding February
    sobbing,   blustering
it's lachrymose way
into virginally
uncooperative March.

Half in love
with easeful Death
who will take
    away this thing
that make us
play at being human.

Weddings & death

      are expensive, complicated, & messy.
People gather who dislike you
    as much as you them.
Paperwork & state registration
    tax changes & new rules
      food, flowers, & fancy dress
open bar or embalming fluid
    someone always leaves pissed.
Feuds start, dreams end,
    & virginities are lost.
Usually organized by
    the one family member
who wouldn't know a bad move
      if it humped their leg.

The one & truly most humane
    difference, is inability
      to marry in your sleep.

Autopsy

I washed my hands before I started
the y-incision had hesitation marks
like a first year med-student under judgmental eyes
slicing cartilage joining ribs to breastbone
was cathartic
using kitchen scissors from expensive knife set
you gave me for our anniversary
check every organ for defect
weighted them in mixing bowls on bathroom scale
wrapped them in sealable bags

used your power saw to open the skull
knowing you hate a messy kitchen
went to backyard to eliminate spatter
spent longer time examining this organ—
no telling sign of defect
no mysterious ridges, dead white zones,
or bloody aneurisms
no reason whatsoever for
why I allow you to kill me
a little more with each blow

Autumn did not come this year

        there is much conjecture and rumination
as to why
but it is hard to focus
the heat a dead weight.
The fall, a time of holding things close
arms filled with corn cobs, pumpkins
groceries for family meals.
I hold nothing
need the air to circulate
freely around me, no more hugging
not even air kisses
the effort is too much.
We do not touch
sleep far apart on moist sheets
their pale blue forget-me-nots wilted.
Winter will not come with its gaiety
hot chocolate and snuggling before fires.
There is a great deal of blame and finger
pointing over global warming, lack of autumn.
All I know for sure is that hell on Earth
is not a figure of speech
for I have received a life sentence.

What came first, the chicken

    A poem in two voices

  or the egg?
In Judeo-Christian-Muslim ethic
it would be the chicken, as God

              (I believe the waitress was first,
                      then his secretary)

created the animals in the garden;
life was good. They received names
there was nice weather, then man

              (friends tell me it's not important;
                but for me it's vital to know exactly
                    what happened, when)

fell and death came to earth.
Animals dying off needed replenishment
so procreation was added to the mix
thus the egg followed the chicken.

              (logic in this situation is a chocolate
                frying pan or Zimbabwean
                      government stock)

In the creationist point of view
there was a single cell which split
into groups forming amoebas
then bigger and different animals.

              (I'm not so stupid if it was pure love
                in the beginning and then went
                      wrong.)

Given that an egg is a single cell
fertilized by another organism
it would seem the egg was first.

                (But if he was banging a bridesmaid
                   in the cloakroom then he needed to die)

A good Buddhist will tell you neither
exists, as they are visual perceptions
or manifestations of unschooled thought.

                (The funeral was a love and shove
                            him affaire)

The chicken that I see
and the egg that I taste
are not the same for you.

                (Now I've got all the time in the
                  world to decide what comes next)

The best way to a man's heart

after Laurell Hamilton

      is six inches of tempered steel
briskly applied between his ribs.
Oh, four or five inches might
get the job done
but to be exact
you need six.
Ironic how phallic objects
are more desirable
the longer they are.
Anyone, who says size
doesn't matter
has been using
knives that are far too short.

she sculpted

        copies of Michelangelo's
David   therapist
prescribed art
to help work through

her issues
as a nod to the prim
she added a leaf

floral codpiece   upon
closer inspection   reveals
poison ivy
growing bolder
a shy coil of
poison sumac snaking
up one leg and
across the buttocks
smiling quietly   she
muses how healing art
can be

After many a summer dies the swan

In gradually strengthening light
we stroll the beach, read, write
grade papers, edit yet again.
In the evening, by the fire
I notice tiny sigh, glance
and wonder, feel I am
a planet tipped off axis
by unfathomable cosmic incident.
Rotating normally now will cause
tectonic shifts in what
I assumed was bedrock.

You only said you needed
      to get back to town.

Can't

The poet mentor
says you can't write
about love, Christmas, or the soul.

First two are overdone
and soul is too vague.

But they have not
seen you naked in rain
chased drops.

Nor have they experienced
exploring with their tongues
while unbuttoning your shirt
all the wild abandon
of Christmas morning

or felt the pain
of closing topaz eyes
fixed and staring.

Hope has no conscience

Autumn leaves shimmer
with silver tears. The cry
of train whistles eerily distinct
the depot noises attenuated
between ice pellets.

I'm dazzled as he materializes
from mists of Dublin train station
enveloped in halo of improbable light.

The other passengers move away
prey's instinctive recognition
of predator in designer suit.

Sometimes we think people are
lottery tickets, there to make
our wildest dreams come true.

I hold out the brown envelope
from private investigator.
He searches my eyes realizing
anything that might
occur to him has already occurred
to me.

I walk home slowly through
the park. Icicles
adorn jaws of statures

as though crying.
That is more than I have.

pourri means rotten in French

I stand in the
    harsh light
pull still moist
    petals
from orchids, gardenias

he loves me
    he slept with her
he bedded several

place petals into Waterford
    crystal so clear
and bright, potpourri pungent
    not unlike sweaty
gleaming bodies
it's good to keep busy

A green removal van or why I cannot love you

after Beth Woods

I am haunted
because distance from desire
is a myth of time.

This box of trinkets
    missives, ticket stubs
        taunts remember

& oh yeah
how his shoulder
  feels under your tongue
his thighs
  under your hands.
Dusty, half-hidden mementos
that should have been ditched
long before this move.
Write out city town state
     on wedding invitation.

Fleeting kisses

There is creative reading as well as creative writing

— Ralph Waldo Emerson

The neon invite

after William Carlo Williams

So much depends
upon

Red neon
light

Flickering with electric
seizures

Beside the two-story
walk-up

Common sense packed a bag on the third cocktail

Way past silly decision
I find myself naked in the afternoon.

It was years since I've been
here, a lifetime,
it was yesterday.

But this is different
since he dropped
his clothes
who says there's no
applause in sex.

New lover

more ambitious
than knowledgeable

I guide
   his hands
      shift his legs

leave him
   breathing gently
soft morning light

only to have him
     surface here
in middle
   of my poem

Love poems for cannibals

how our linguistic ability
will foil us
in the time of cannibals

bite me, eat me
felled by an
ambiguous antecedent

Spaceman Dave

      claims the void
is full of stars

your hand outstretched
light beams launch
from stone facets
no less a voice

after all my universe
only what I can affect
is full of hot nights

Moment

after Alan Britt

a frog strangling
rain
washes out
my Sweet Williams

outside magic
is made by weather moves

inside electricity
builds, crackling
with cinnamon
candles overflowing

Clay bodies

clay on spinning wheel
wobbles, tilts
firm hands slender fingers

jolly a moving dream
make it stable
sustainable

oven fires, sets
a vessel
that is better than before
filled with ideas
yearning

don't remember when

    I first invented you
with me
sent a prayer
into frigid raw world

along winding temporal river
that comes now to rest
content on your shoulders
sparkles briefly

illuminated by candlelight
winks wickedly
as you lower your body
onto mine

Editorial

for the Australian Poets

a foreigner sends
me his words
such speech is magic
his thoughts, ideas
course through
cause shudders
as if
a host of celestial doves
flutter inside my ribs
a stranger
with writing like that
I wonder what breakfast
will taste like
off his chest

By the way

        I have lain
with the wolf
in verdure forest

the one you warn
fervently against

Forgive me
he was strong
warm
his tongue a rasp

A rose by

He
calls
me
Princess
and
I am.

Magic

circling   orbits
two bodies

resilient, old energy
dangerously close
to sentience
  which it proves
    by trying to hold still
      so as not to be noticed

pressure builds threating
plate glass windows
    wine glasses
crackling and swirling
in the corner
porcelain Kuan Yin giggles

the eastern clouds

        are angel wings
spread for flight
the clouds in the west
are crumpled sheets
you & I
in the middle
are concerned with more
concrete images
such as the curve of your lips
& your using them to rewrite
our history

I have no dowry

sheep or goats
land or title

there is no juicy portfolio
no stocks, bonds
secret Cayman account

I have little or nothing
between me and & penury
but words

and with these
I've made you
the desire of lovers
far and wide
until a time
of no poetry

If by chance

        I could write a universe
into a single
poem
in a cosmos filled
with tens of millions
an endless necropolis
of poetry by persons
bereft of soul
feeling al the wiser
the more unknowing
of what or where
they came or went
I'd still write
about the way it feels
entering a room
and your blue eyes
alighting as they spy me

Behavior of waves

did you know the waves
off one coast
are entirely unlike those
of any other place
   like sex
      and poetry

simple, with limited number
of ways to compose

yet I can name a poet
     by third stanza
recognize
   touch of your hand
in darkness

know feel of your weight
rhythms of movement

the surf off Donegal
or flying with angels

Wanton Disarray

They sicken of the calm who know the storm.
        — Dorothy Parker, Sunset Fun: Poems

All I want is a kiss

      that invites envy
but no awkwardness
from those who see

irresistible pull
    impossible to escape

a fleeting moment where there is
no time
no spin of planet
no gravitational wave born of Big Bang

to burn with singular intensity
      those who were lost
      now anchored
      at reality's edge

if all existence implodes
in that instant
I will patiently reassemble
the molecules of the universe—
particle by particle
for just that moment

before I drown in life

After T. S. Eliot

certain half-deserted streets
one-night cheap hotels
of insidious intent
men come and go
rubbing backs

on window-pane sheets
flicking tongues into possibilities
returning to soot
which falls from chimneys
where families abide

there will be time
to prepare a face
to create and murder
a hundred indecisions
evening, morning, afternoon
time for half-truths to eyes
that fix you, pinned
wriggling

but I have known arms
perfume of sweat
smoothed by long fingers
I have wept and fasted
wept and prayed
was it worth
sniggers:

talk of you and me

after sunsets, novels
coffee cups
to say what I mean
a bit obtuse
almost ridiculous
but I grow old and
need just once
to live

When I'm alone

I want you
   to take my clothes
off   slowly
   on a Cornish cliff

waves of grasses
   no moon

tonight, but now it's noon
and your mouth

finds mine

fragile blue sky
sunlight breakable and thin

shooting glassy shards
through closed eyelids

the gulls become quiet
in reverence and heat

is no competition
   for butterflies
that tickle my breasts

and you

match ocean's rhythm
such a beautiful time

to share, if I ever
get to meet you

Bookstore

A long slow tea-shoppe-lit English afternoon
and the bench opposite the book store
is blessedly empty. From its far-left side
one can observe store owner
the sly hinge of my desire.

                      His hands
caress bindings, stroke pages
softly sighs when perfection
is perceived. Behind & around him,
rows of doors;
to fairylands,
Mars,
& barns filled with love-sick cowboys.

                      His body
was carved late at night
in moonlight, by an absent-minded archangel
who did not know when to stop. Books
heavy as centuries, heavy as this knot in my gut
start to look like rows
of gritted teeth
keeping me at bay.

                Tomorrow I will conquer
that shop door
tomorrow and tomorrow
stretches out
a series of padlocks.

Fall, falling, fell

I ran from the train station
busy streets, stiff breeze,
sidewalk café, diminutive tables
white-washed, scrolled wrought iron,
empty cake plates frosting dabs and crumbs,
heavily wrapped and coated friends
braving weather to remain apart from bourgeoisie.
All of them laughing and a stranger
in long grey coat, blue eyes,
a scarlet leaf perched on his shoulder
golden, amber and bronze leaves
scattered jewels, adorn the scene.
The world stops for a nanosecond
to spin again so fast
I fall into chair—
some hellos
hurt more
than a hundred goodbyes.

I have met a regrettable for instance

Built of left over angles and extra-long parts
someone forgot to give him a coat of paint.
But he recites Houseman's *Land of Lost Content*
over Guinness and his eyes are blue.
When he walks I think his knees should bend
backwards. Spiky hair is blond while I like
dark haired men except he plays classical
guitar and knows who Pat Metheny is.
Too young and too fast, he read
at Cambridge and plays chess in Classical
Latin. He is a moment
that will not let me catch my breath.
I look for tears that are not flowing
and know it is only a matter of time
with this rogue less traveled.

All he said was hello

the universe opens   skies fall
galaxies spin   deserts flood
the Medusa Cascade changes color
nebulas condense into suns
suns collapse into black hopes
comets lose their endless battle
    with gravities' forces
destroying massive worlds
here   in this space
        my universe
          my memory
preserved in mental lucite
      or asleep in a bed in New Orleans
overwhelmed by first sight
shatters

the gravitational wave
released by Big Bang
finally reaches Earth

The first time

        a woman undresses a man
her hands shake, grappling
tiny buttons, smaller holes.
Her own body's senses assaulted
by his lips, touch
the breeze as her own
clothes drop to carpet.
Every zipper a Herculean challenge
disorientation from the magic
of smooth sin, brush of fingertips
spell of mystery, surprise.
A miracle only once
this speaking
in secrets and sweets.

A thousand times you will try to recreate this.

But eventually even the memory
will be nothing more than
a whisper of lips
remembered on rainy days

Mother said I would be safe

        so long as I kept to the path
but sometimes the path winds
through dark places.

The well–trod dirt
poses no thrills

while gold and scarlet leaves
make a trail into trees whose branches
reach out to hug

breeze whispers crazy secrets.
In this basket
I have a bottle of wine

warm bread and fragrant cheese
know rumors regarding wolves
strong arms of woodsmen

in the deep blue distance—
blue as the heart of flame—
red is the color of danger.

Practice

his lips were soft hibiscus
I kissed more than one
kind of flower—
best way to practice—

a spark inside
blossoms flame
vines snake
kudzu through me
to my lips

his lips magnolias
        driftwood
                sound of ocean in my ears

when he steps back
we stand
    on the same path
and yet a different one

Snow

we made snow angels
pair after pair
across the meadow
until it appeared a giant ogre
stomped through in the night

laughing and frostbit
we staggered home
to shower.
Fireplace, hot chocolate
nothing reaches the glacier within

then we make sheet angels
melting under us
spreading heat turning
mountain snow to torrential tides

cascading into valley below
while people in town
look on in awe

#2

nurse presses mask in place,
says, *Go to your happy place*

I think of that small patch
  of skin on your shoulder
  where the crest begins

  its cascade

to the plateau of chest
  musk
    aftershave
      detergent
mingle

vie with scented candles
I alone know

the taste of this
muscles ripple as you move

to cradle me
a separate entity to my lips
a place to nip

  lick
before resting my head
the trip down high plains
takes time
preparation
drugs make a thundering

sound in my head
wash me

straight into dreams of you.

The days go by

Found poetry – Albert Goldbarth

we've all seen a lover
    and walked up to a stranger
we've all leapt on a lover
    and rolled off a stranger
I may not be a lady of the court
    come from parrots and cakes
but I know the nubbin inside
      that lets out length after length
          of this delicate filament seen…

science fiction is full of these distances
    quasar travel
the world is hollow, its blood dance hallowed
and during distilling of lavender and citron
nights go by   seeing faces of lovers
in sleep of elsewhere, maybe with another lover
we lay by the breathing of strangers
   we've seen the faces return
      from the spaces so vast
          light fails   words fail   maybe distance is
only a night

I am surrounded by the mundane
    a paperweight   bowl of plums   blank journal
austere shell with only slightest blush
of vulva pink inside it
It's raining   violet and soft
        the kind of shadows cast by worn flannel

in the corner you sigh in your sleep   turn slightly   weary
you're not giving up   my lover remains in my bed
night   sightless night goes by   it happens that way

whole air around him in pictures   words I've yet to write
     light is a gallery   nothing he does will ever be lost

in a frenzied moment

        Juliet tryst I
gave myself to know
your weight on me
your smell on my skin

in time usually given
to moans
rash promises
or false declarations
you whisper
if an alternate universe
spins off from a decision
you will be
bound in my embrace
looping eternally
on the river surface of time

this vision is my life raft
when the river
threatens to pull me under

I must wake you

my lips keen   to lick your shoulder
    my lust   a needle playing
you, the groove   with sweet song

    a taste
on my tongue   fresh as morning stalls
at farmer's market   sharp as cheese and leeks

      wild as hare

a slice of light reclines
    on your bare thighs   I am jealous
so many things   we have not done
    so many regrets we will have

      from the wasted time
this sleep

When I take you in my mouth   soft as brie   this candle
    hardens
       half floats
    in sleep   so gently sails to fulfilled dreams

Hold and kiss me until the dawn

curtains flutter occasionally
as they remember job description
you stretch across rumpled bed sheets
one arm on your face
my lips are sticky
from peach slices
you fed me
daubing juice on nipples
between breasts
licking it, in time
to slip another pale slice in my mouth
followed by kisses so hot
I taste peach flambé

as you work your wiles
I find myself pining for you
inches away, yet never
quite here and I wait
for you to come home
from travels
in your mind
or where you think you should be
when I ask what your dreams are
you tell me they are balloon juice

from the radio, Candi Stanton sings,
"he called me Baby, Baby, Baby
all night long"

and I long for night;
you asleep
quiet in my arms, finally home

But when I kiss you

when I kiss him
I worry about

    my breath
    where we are
    where we will be
    & when

try to remember

        when I shaved my legs
        which underwear I've got on

        if I shut off my phone
            TV, computer

decide if I want
    to stop
    go on
    or dangle

But when I kiss you

it all stops
    my breath
    my thoughts
    earth's rotation

even deities pause
  to watch
    remember
I hope they catch me as I fall

Birds and bees, Part 2

Slow northern light breaks
tentative rays tease
open magenta folds
of Prairie Blazing Star
bumble bee alights
seeking morning moisture
rest before days' endeavors
slipping into little groove
which treasures pollen sac
a slight tickle for flower.
Does it stand a little straighter?
Bee drinks its fill
leaves tiny message
from the universe
takes a love note
for another flower
another time.

an Giblean*

Diamond month of my birth
a brink, ledge, one step away
from pure potential spread out before me, us
a fresco unfurling with whorls and color curves
selkies sliding into sea waters
fairy rings of shuddering green
raspberries and loganberries dangle pregnant
from moaning vines
a sparkling pearl peeking from grey oyster shell
couple waltzing on beach under a spoon-tip moon
I do not want to sleep
waste time on non-productive activity
but remember old adage
when you can't sleep, you're in someone else's dreams

Yet this April, the finest of many
 is not a dream, too perfect
to nail down, too rich to be illusion

*Gaelic for April

Didn't know I was starving until I tasted you

Three snowy days makes delicious crunch
beneath our boots, lovely and soft
piled on roofs and corners
of mullioned windows, icing
on gingerbread houses.

A bright sun
finally remembers his job
glistens off cottages lavishly
painted pie-case colors:
    lemon here, hint of strawberry
        glimpse of pistachio
            with sudden splash of peach cobbler.

The street glitters
    sunlight nearly blinding.
It seems we are
walking between gumdrops
to a chocolate inn where russet stone
has turned mahogany.
It's doors open in welcome.

Giggle through sign-in, we rush
to snowy sheets
    the past
        another country now.
The present
    is finding candy sweets
        with hands and lips,
a fast pouring nectar

of discovery and bliss.

Our future filled
with insatiable appetites.

Appetites vary

Coffee fragrance gets my attention.
Sparrow hops lawn stopping
head cocked,   dives under pottery
worm jerked roughly into flight.
Neighbor's cat goes forth—
    field mouse clutched in teeth.

I've eaten strange and wonderful things.

A certain gentleman from San Antonio
    left a taste
on my tongue   new as mint released penny
    first drop of plum tomatoes

I sucked on his biceps   in Fort Worth
made a feast of his abs   in Oklahoma
    negligees
        tossed in many corners.

Dappling light   slides across kitchen floor
    I think how lovely   inside of his thighs
will be

with my toast.

Where two curves meet

I stroke his face
smooth his eyebrows
smiling dents at corners of mouth
his face pliant and flowing
under my fingers
I feel I can shape him.

My hands wander
playing hide and seek
with blankets edge
he stretches like a cat
and my hand
bumps his penis
blossoming in time-lapse photography

He disturbs the air
draws near breaking
it into tense ripples of silence
that holds its breath

When you wake the world
will be ninety-three
and one fourth degrees off normal
teetering on cusp.

A poetic light

I rise early try to capture
perfect poem
that fled on cat feet as I woke.
Six lines into mental musings

a curious ray of north light
finds your calf
softly caressing relaxed muscles
as through its travels—
of millions of miles—
was launched for this destination.

Tiny sparkles dance down beam
because here is magic.
My writing urge yields
to different desire knowing
its violent need a juxtaposition
to inquisitive patch
now slyly
moving up your thigh.

My hands remember how it feels
in the dark, my fingers itch
to detect change of brilliance and warmth;
my lips yearn to taste. Before
these feelings overwhelm
light beam drops
into area framed by sheets and one leg
pulled up to chest.

The end of a rainbow
a pot of gold.
How lucky I feel
as I slide back into bed
to claim my treasure.

Bolt from the blue

hike gone awry, night
catches us out past curfew

spoon-tip moon mocks
until a rapid darkness

overwhelms and dry lighting
puts on show

accompanying wind brings
taste of petrichor

we seek shelter, rock outcrop
but dragon breath air

finds us and jagged lights
reflect in your eyes

with insidious intent
as you pull my t-shirt

off, you tell me
to count backwards from infinity

when I reach the last 4 numbers
in Pi, lightning strikes

my middle, my heart
synchronizes with thunder

in the morning, two buzzards
perch nearby, both heads tilted

same direction, their potential
noonday meal laughing

almost too hard
to get dressed

Speaking of boiled eggs,
I'm not wearing pajama bottoms

Potato salad, company picnic
caused three days of the wobbles
and green apple dirties.
That lift home stranded
us both: you too ill to go further
and me
too sick to be pretty. We pass, zombies in hall
giving regular obeisance
to a clichéd god.

But a gentle autumn sun
has risen
to calmer, quieter household.
We smile and nod
over tea and toast
you in my pink chenille bathrobe
and me, in pajama top.

I begin to wonder.

Are you strong enough
for me to make you forget.
My vice is perfectly primed

Maybe a shower together
    and if
 you're too weak
I'll take the top.

Here have a bit more toast
we need to build up your strength.

It's been too long or why I'm not allowed in Kroger

blinding sunlight broken by air conditioning
aroma of dirt   produce & red pick-up trucks
alstroemeria &   roses   pungent carnations & phlox

   silvery, mylar balloons fastened   restrained   tied
apples, red, green   sweet & tart   spells   lips   prince's kiss

garlic, onions   concentrate on list
  plums rest in my palm   firm & tight
juicy, undulating apricots
      rusticated rhubarb   unyielding   hard

lettuce   leaves fainting painting   stories of friendly flora
   cauliflower   Rubenesque cherries
zucchini & squash   elongated & curved

strawberries   blackberries   whipped crème
cucumbers   oiled   glossy
automatic shower   moist   slick ....

hunting

days have spun into weeks
months walking this forest
skipping, singing torch songs
still my love has not shown
neither pulled my blouse off shoulder
nor split my riding cape

only woodsmen beckon me

today I dab beef blood
on wrists and knees
drop cuts of raw steak
behind me

as I traverse darkened foliage
slowly brush bush and bark
now I hear his panting
see his shining brown eyes
as I recline beneath branches
which shut out the sun
feel leaves around me shift, sigh
he comes

    my beloved

        he comes

How invisibility works

Children cover their faces
squeeze their eyes tight
believe this makes them invisible.

I keep trying. Strain my eyelids
tight until bright colors
rocket through my head
with vapor tail of pain.

Face in hands
you should not be able
to see me
no one should
but you slowly

pull my hands away—
peek-a-boo never so fun
as with one who sees

past the package
to the part never seen
by the rabble.

champagne shoulders

caramel colored hair
    and milk chocolate eyes

I am hungry
    and evening so far away
        dream of snacking

nibbles of hard jaw line
    lead to insatiable tongue
        flicks on neck

sipping champagne shoulders
    sample non-peril nipples

sprinkles of confetti
    leave Hansel and Gretel trail

to hard candy center
    watch gelatin shivers

as I run fingers lightly
    up appetizing thighs

notice eyes melt as I
    sate my hunger

A ticklish thing, anticipation

He saw the dress
in vintage clothing store window
across Yorkshire high street.
Tea colored, Victorian, high-neck.
Although he had no idea
of such terms.

It was
the seemingly hundred
tiny buttons marching
down the back that gave him—
what was proving to be—
a very painful erection.

Deep cuffs, sported
yet more button rows
forcing him to shift in café chair.
The thought of slowly
working his way
through sweet agony
to reach yielding skin
softly scented, frangipani.

He brings it up at dinner
tries to keep it casual
but obvious fidgeting betrays
physical distress.
High street, next day

I find the wedding dress
small alterations needed.
Serious shopping provides
high top, button shoes
with wicked button hook.
Search finished with ribbon-laced bustier

individual ribbons, I will make
sure Bridesmaid double knots.

Pack them with jasmine scented paper
wait patiently
for him to recognize
as I float down the aisle.

Headlong

The moon was on fire
      & a line of fair hair

meandered
   down his belly
Road to Gethsemane

which I travel
  slowly, stopping
at points of interest

until a Crab Nebula
    forms
           at my core
   reaches electrical

tentacles   into previously

  unknown crevasses

     breath taking telescopic

there is nothing like
the taste of sugar
after the taste of sex

Whimsy

Somewhere, maybe between fourth
    & fifth beer
I lean over   place a linguolabial trill

(read zerple)

on his cheek. After all, what is life
    without whimsy?

His hands   catch my face
he places   ale flavored kiss
on my surprised lips.

After clothes   stumbling   duvet
    giggling   groping   evoking
the deity

we bask in happy stupor
    I find sweet spot
        between fourth & fifth rib
& blow an extended raspberry
    of implied satisfaction

I find it easy

      to get drunk on words
in fact I am rarely sober

but your voice a mixture
bourbon, Dublin butter and sex

your words — the moon flying
a storm-driven ships

a sea of clouds — even this
diatribe on misplacement

of an apostrophe has me
squirming, nipples hard

as I try to concentrate
yet all I think is

wanting you to write a poem
on my back in chocolate.

Singing in the dark

He takes my words
lonely and scared
eases them into rhythm
beat
covers imperfections
with forceful bridge
even our disagreements
dissonance and sour notes
fit, masterpiece
of chorus
and I know this man
is the only instrument
through which my music
can be heard.

She asked what you are like

      he's science explained
by artists   poets
something beautiful
    that makes no sense

when his lips find
mine
   there's the silence
of a thousand
   unvisited museums

I close my eyes
   to a deep red
     alternating
first flash of morning
sun or autumn leaves

he's much too wise
      for sand castles
but not for kissing
   my breasts in elevators.

I sat back, sipped coffee
exhausted, as she says
I've not described you at all.

Those who wander are not lost

For Tobi & Jeff Alfier

The coffee gets stronger
and his sighs longer
when the wander urge
comes upon him.
As much as I love and need him
he must go roaming.

His mistress, his camera
will capture
      conjure the world
           reduce it   to pixilated
dreams of another life.

He says I'm free
to come or go
    to another,
has no idea how my insides burn,
head swims when he talks
    such nonsense.

Go, I say, *I'll be here*
    waiting for fresh views
exciting as Christmas morning.

Find me something red
he gives me last hug sideways
    most of him
        already out the door.

He stops, conflicted
    I keep you too much in rust
      cracked windows
        and shadowed, dirty doorways.

Yes, my heart has been beautifully tied.

Of Christmases to come

We argue where to spend Christmas:
under the Eiffel Tower, Dublin or Skye.
And I can't understand
why it matters
as long as I can see
those blue eyes, warm grin.

His words are gaily wrapped
radiance written
in my own heart's blood
able to lift the dead in their vaulted arches.
Hand in hand we walk leaves
dirty brown and crackly beneath our feet
twisted bare limbs reach out to grasp
our warmth, life. But we are protected

by a shield unseen. Older couples pass
details of their faces worn smooth
doubtful like salutes
of cemetery angels worn, eroded by time.
Someday that will be us, mellowed by
joys and sorrows yet to come;
this exciting, edgy love assuming
a patina of comforting assurance.

About the author

Wanton Disarray is Michelle Hartman's fourth book. Her other works, *Irony and Irreverence, Disenchanted and Disgruntled*, & *Lost Journal of My Second Trip to Purgatory*, are available on Amazon. Hartman's work can be found online, in multiple journals here, and various countries overseas. She is the former editor of Red River Review and holds a BS degree in Political Science, Pre-Law from Texas Wesleyan University and a Paralegal Cert. from Tarrant County College. She was recently named a Distinguished Alumni by Tarrant County College.

www.ingramcontent.com/pod-product-compliance
Lightning Source LLC
Chambersburg PA
CBHW031205090426
42736CB00009B/795